PEACE

Rhythm of My Heart

Thupten Tendhar

Center for Nonviolence & Peace Studies
The University of Rhode Island
74 Lower College Rd. MCC 202
Kingston, RI 02881, USA

First Edition, 2013

ISBN 978-0-615-82774-2

Cover photos & design: Thupten Tendhar
Author's photograph: Indrawati Liauw

"Love and compassion are necessities, not luxuries. Without them humanity cannot survive."

H.H. The Dalai Lama

Table of Contents

Foreword

By Paul Bueno de Mesquita, PhD

If the journey to peace in our world truly begins within each of us then finding the source of inner peace must become our first step. Thupten Tendhar journeyed to our Center for Nonviolence and Peace Studies at the University of Rhode Island in the summer of 2008 wearing only his scarlet robe, open sandals and a large, endearing smile, a bright and inviting symbol of his enormous compassionate spirit. He came to participate in the annual International Nonviolence Summer Institute in order to study the principles and methodology of nonviolence according to Dr. Martin Luther King, Jr. From day one we realized that we were going to learn far more from him than we could ever teach him. And so it has been.

Most of us are never taught the lessons of inner peace in our formal schooling. Lessons that are so necessary for our very survival and essential to our overall well being are rarely taught to us. We must learn them on our own through experience and self-reflection during our emotional life journey. Through self realization and awareness we open ourselves to these most important lessons. These we must learn by heart and keep with us for a lifetime. The conditions of self-reflection and self-awareness needed for learning by heart the lessons of inner peace can be found in the pages of this small volume of poetry. These heartfelt images and emotional revelations are brought to us from across the centuries, handed down to us by a poetic messenger emerging out of the cloak of ancient contemplative monastic traditions.

Meaningful and deeply felt emotions are portrayed through the simplicity of every day surroundings and experiences. The mastery of empathic sensitivity and a compassionate tenderness touches our interconnectedness with ourselves, with others, and with the beauty of observing our natural world. Using a style of authentic expression in free form structure, the words and images flow together often in a repetitive chant-like cadence. In writing a foreword, one is to propose the purpose of the book that follows and to explain the goal of the author's work. But from these pages there appears no ulterior motive, no esoteric goals, no abstract purpose, only the sharing of one bodhisattva's journey through life as he follows the rhythm of his heart beating a path toward inner peace. If you listen carefully with an open heart you too will hear the rhythm of the chant, feel the pulse in each present moment, and take another small step toward your own enlightenment ❖

I. Peace & Harmony

Create a Better World

What if all conflicts are resolved?

What if every yell is silenced?

What if entire families are reunited?

What if all broken hearts are soothed?

What if every missile is disarmed?

What if all bombs are defused?

What if all enemies are reconciled?

What if every war is ended?

What if guns are loaded with roses?

What if cries are transformed into melody?

What if tortures are stopped?

What if sad feelings are erased?

What if stones of ego are ground down?

What if arrows of humiliation are broken?

What if holes of depression are filled?

What if the fetors of stress are freshened?

What if suspicions are flattened?

What if jealousy is melted?

What if threats are quarantined?

What if terrorism is wiped out?

What if harsh words are eliminated?

What if hatred minds are expelled?

What if selfish attitudes are eradicated?

What if wrong views are righted?

What if hungers are fed?

What if thirsts are quenched?

What if shivers are clothed?

What if the poor are respected?

What if animals are befriended?

What if the environment is protected?

What if wildfires are prevented?

What if everybody shoulders responsibility?

What if the trees grow fresh green hair?

What if the sky cheers its turquoise face?

What if stars twinkle their golden eyes?

What if flowers blossom their vibrant smiles?

What if the earth yields nontoxic foods?

What if the rivers flow clean water?

What if the oceans evaporate for needed rain?

What if the sun and moon shine without clouds?

What if the mountains stand without melting?

What if the ozone stretches without wounds?

What if we renounce altering our ecology?

What if we realize harming others harms ourselves?

What if the children are taught peace?

What if the parents nurture absolute love?

What if teachers practice great compassion?

What if nonviolence is rewarded to all?

What if a big smile greets everybody?

What if a calm look adorns each face?

What if a warm heart enriches every mind?

What if strong arms embrace everyone?

What if loving kindness becomes universal?

What if people survive on infinite peace?

What if the Media finds no more dreadful stories?

What if we open a fresh new world?

What if every individual thinks for society?

What if the society takes care of individuals?

What if freedom exceeds cell phone coverage?

What if laughter roars louder than car engines?

What if the legislatures structure law for peace?

What if the executives run offices in harmony?

What if judges conduct hearings for justice?

What if serenity and prosperity glitter for all?

What if we cherish life more than materials?

What if we respect others more than oneself?

What if we convert battlegrounds into lovelands?

What if we applaud peace more than violence?

What if my rumbling words turn into action?

What if my childish dreams become real?

What if my global happy wishes are fulfilled?

What if you help me Create a Better World?

A Big Smile for Peace, Please

We face global warming

We suffer from high blood pressure

We witness wars and campus shootings

Thus, we use heavy makeup.

There is a glowing beauty within us

It just needs to be revealed

Be at peace every day

And, smile at everyone you meet.

Host No Hate

Your heart is an ocean

Float no hate on it

Your mind is a garden

Grow no hate in it

Your body is a charisma

Adorn no hate on it

Your voice is a melody

Tune no hate in it

Your life is a journey

Escort no hate with it

Your day is a paradise

Light no hate in it

Your night is a galaxy

Launch no hate in it

Your sleep is a magic

Dream no hate in it

Your food is a delicacy

Spice no hate in it

Your sport is a delight

Shout no hate in it

Your school is a family

Enroll no hate in it

Hate hate, if you have to hate.

Tank Crossing

Flowers no more to be seen

Music no more to be heard

Smiles no more to be enjoyed

For tanks are crossing

Jungle no more is exploratory

Water no more is portable

Air no more is breathable

For tanks are rolling

Birds no more to be watched

Camels no more to be ridden

Fishes no more to be fed

For tanks are invading

Playgrounds no more are safe

Games no longer are fun

Friends not many are left

For tanks are firing

Fathers, time to wage nonviolence

Mothers, time to protect children

Together, to pledge and assure

That tanks don't run over your kids.

8/20/2011, Providence, RI Airport

Peace is what I can dedicate the most,

Yet, Peace is what I miss.

Peace is what I beg you the most,

Peace is what I encourage you the most,

Peace is why I respect you the most,

Peace is the holiness I see in you.

URI Center for Nonviolence & Peace Studies, Kingston, RI

One Summer Night

Sitting by a bonfire

Sipping a root beer

Facing the cool breeze

Gazing at the clear sky

I saw a shiny galaxy of stars

that reminded me of my father

who called the stars by names

and predicted weather quite often

by stars and the moon's phases

to cultivate his small farm

or to walk out on a pilgrimage tour

but those seasons are passed, I realized.

An airplane stole my mind that moment

Blinking its amber and green lights

It left me to ponder and wonder thus,

Whose daughters were flying?

And who else was in transit?

Each must be somebody's darling

Mother or father, wife or husband

Son or daughter, boyfriend or girlfriend

Brother or sister, far far away

Like me, wandering in the space

Dreaming for the best

Silently, curiously, but caringly

My mind hugged them all

Saying '*Bon Voyage*'

Sharing his best wishes

Sending all the warm prayers

For their life's safety

And reunion with dear ones

No matter whom they are—

Male or female, young or old

Spiritualists or atheists

Literate or illiterate—

To expand love to build harmony

To add meanings to generate peace

So everybody will be happy.

The bonfire died down

The summer-night grew colder

Some mosquitoes began singing

And the bats started their party

My belly was happy with delicacy

Yet, my eyes were itching for sleep

I thanked angels for the amazing night

And rejoiced great days with them

Muchas Gracias!!

Francis Horn Drive, Kingston, RI

Violence or Nonviolence

Emotional disruption

Verbal misconduct

Physical craziness

Intellectual blindness

Causing disrespect.

Endless fights

Merciless tortures

Costly bombardments

Heartless shootings

Bloody killings.

Leaving hundreds of widows

Creating thousands of orphans

Wounding millions of hearts

Inflicting billions of pains

Destroying centuries of trusts.

Slashing friendship

Sowing racism

Growing hate

Fueling terrorism

And evolving violence.

What do we need?

All those scraps

Or simply nonviolence

To live a happy life

And to let others live happily.

Violence - The Toxic Step

I see some strong men and women

Carrying guns as they go out to hunt

Leavng families they suffer days and nights

Crossing jungles they step out forever

With each step they deposit trauma

With each footprint they imprint toxin

With each breath they sense uncertainty

Alas! Anger and hatred trap them forever.

Every voice of anger echoes thrice

Every footprint of hate grows tenfold

Every act of killing multiplies by hundreds

Yet some walk violence, the Toxic Step

Courageous ones I appeal to you to imagine

Melody of compassion echoing thrice

Flowers of love blooming tenfold

And remedy of nonviolence healing cries

Watch every stride you make on the earth

Hear every noise you release in the air

Feel every print you leave on the heart

Be it nontoxic always, for goods' sake!

Ruthless Winter & War

Winter, the heartless, has landed.

Turmoil jolts again.

Innocent millions perish.

The ultimate outcome is chilling.

Disgust flows down.

The poor wait hungry for days.

They have no sympathy to warm them,

And do not know how to avoid the madness.

Mothers lose sons

Fathers lose daughters.

Shedding tears and energies, they search.

But many are lost forever.

Look how heartless the winter is,

How awful the bombardment is.

The beautiful meadows have turned gray.

Alas! No way to survive, wretched plants.

I watched from a lookout far away

Trees struggling for life,

All the flowers dying in pain.

Can you feel the agony of the poor?

There is suffering 24/7

Cries and miseries pollute the ozone;

Death tolls pile up like snow on mountains.

The whole earth is turned into a graveyard.

There may be sunshine soon. I hope.

Warm salute to you, our precious spring.

Restore the strong flow of cool streams.

Let peace adorn our ailing globe. Please.

Let fish thrive in joy and

The lotus amuses us with full-blossom.

Swans display the perfection of romance.

What more do we need for a happy life?

Only then can we enjoy the glee,

The clarity of a blue sky,

The charisma of a full moon

The brightness of twinkling stars, and…

We can imagine having fun together,

Friendships that last for a long time.

Satisfaction in spite of position and income,

Smiles as long as you are alive.

Plants grow fresh and green,

Colorful flowers adorn our garden,

Birds sing high at dawn and dusk,

Waves dance gentle at sea shores.

Wild animals inherit their shelter,

Butterflies take their nectar.

There will be a plateful for everybody.

Hunger and thirst become a story from the past.

Love and compassion bind us together;

Families, societies and nations keep flourishing.

Our world transforms into a paradise,

A harmony of spirit and technology.

Environment and inhabitants caring for each
other!

Peace and prosperity any time, everywhere.

That's my dream of a world to live in and pass
through.

Bless me Buddha, Jesus, Allah and Ishvar.

July 26, 2006 Atlanta, GA

A Tarzan Monk

I want to be a Tarzan

A Tarzan in a simple maroon robe

A Tarzan friendly with every being

A Tarzan who smiles forever

I want to be a Tarzan monk

Far away in a remote jungle

Where the aroma of sandalwood prevails

Hymns of nightingales are heard

I want to be a Tarzan monk

The best friend of monkeys

Daring dark caves and wild cats

Caring not about days or dates

I want to be Tarzan monk

To swims across down-falling rivers

To go afar swinging grapevines

And to pound arrogance out of my chest

I want to be a Tarzan monk

One who takes great care of water lilies

An eye witness of birds and animals

Who roam and quench their thirst on lonely
shores

I want to be a Tarzan monk

Who never thirsts for praise or fame

Rather, one who always strives for good

For the sake of others and oneself

I want to be a Tarzan monk

One who is eco-friendly with nature

The Sun would be my source of warmth

And the moon bestows me soothing waves.

I want to be a Tarzan monk

A monk who follows a bee

No matter how steep the river falls

No matter how far the flowers grow

The sweet nectars of beautiful flowers!

The nutritious essence of crystal rivers!

No more may I seek comfort

No more may I be a slave of living

I wish to sit in lotus posture

Through bright days and dark nights

My spine as straight as a young Teakwood

My compassion resting peacefully within

Profundity would be my breathing

Calm would be my mind

Years will pass away swiftly but,

Love and compassion would thrive inside.

Only then, will I be a billionaire

A billionaire of wisdom and compassion

A billionaire who can never be robbed

A billionaire who will rest in peace forever

No anger to produce enmity

No jealousy to cause rivalry

No pride to disrespect others

No ignorance to breed negativity.

Mexico City, Mexico 2002

Spiritual Nourishment

Life is incomparably beautiful

More than a gorgeous lotus

a smiling sunflower

or a colorful daisy.

Constantly it grows to blossom

Should the root remain strong.

Just add some spiritual nectar, dear

So your life will grow wonderfully big.

A life supported well by spirituality

not only grows and flourishes colorful

It also becomes fruitfully sweet

And, is able to stand strong amid tornados.

Enrich yourself with kind spiritual thoughts

Dedicate everything for a very meaningful life

Adorn your soul with infinite love and compassion

Smile, and keep smiling every day, please.

Peace, Peace, Peace!

Be Peace!

Think peace

Speak peace

Act peace

Teach peace

Promote peace

Study peace

Write peace

Create peace

Talk peace

Lead peace

Sanction peace

Wage peace

Sing peace

Dance peace

Enjoy peace

Befriend peace

Inhale peace

Exhale peace

Live peace

Dream peace

Be peace!

I Wish

May every child be cheerful like a spring flower

May every child be open-minded like a vast sky

May every child be lively like the Atlantic Ocean

May every child be majestic like Mount Everest

May every child have a strong body like sandal wood

May every child have lilting speech like a nightingale

May every child have a helping heart like Mother Theresa

May every child have a caring spirit like Mahatma Gandhi

May every child possess the humility of gentle mothers

May every child possess the courage of sturdy fathers

May cvcry child posscss thc cxpcricncc of all elders

May every child possess the wisdom of all teachers

May every child be free from harsh bullying actions

May every child be free from cold segregating hearts

May every child be free from cruel killing weapons

May every child be free from a painful depressed mind

May every child enjoy a feast of peace and freedom

May every child enjoy building a better tomorrow.

II. Freedom & Justice

Longing

Each minute of waiting for you

Lasts more than an hour

And each hour of waiting for you

I suffer longer than a day

The Sun shines in the east

The Moon sneaks to the west

The Sun shines in the west

And the Moon sneaks to the east

Days and nights amass dull

I don't know how am I surviving

Foods sit cold on the table

And I stay awake all night long

Heart cries inside my chest

Tears fall out of my eyes

People take me as a crazy man

Yet, my dream for you is alive

I wait, and will be waiting

Thinking of you each heartbeat

Longing for you every second

Until my dream comes true

All day, all night

Longing for you—freedom!

9/9/11

I have A Dream Too!

I have a dream too

A dream to visit Tibet

To console ailing souls

To light up butter lamps

To turn gigantic prayer wheels

To give alms to the poor

To sing hymns for ancestors

And to repair wrecked stupas.

I have a dream too

A dream to quench thirst

For food and education

Insight and reality

Hope and hobbies

Ideas and planning

Faith and devotion

Love and friendship.

I have a dream too

To embrace the pitiable orphans

To be their good playmate

To bring cheer to their faces

To guide them onto the right path

To enrich their awareness

To assure health and happiness

And to witness their progress.

I have a dream too

A dream for a joyful reunion

Of masters and students

Parents and children

Grandparents and grandchildren

Wives and husbands

Lovers and beloved

Relatives and friends.

I have a dream too

A dream for a Free World

For rights of the people

To express their ideas

For sacred spiritual practices

To uphold precious traditions

To preserve endangered identity

And to choose their leaders.

I have a dream too

To flutter a Peace Flag

On top of the Potala palace and

Peak of snowy mountains

Throughout the world countries

As free as in the United States.

I have a dream too

A dream to rejuvenate Tibet

By replanting countless trees

Minimizing lethal pollution

Setting dammed rivers free

Cleaning the littered facade of the Himalayas

Protecting antelopes and pandas

And restoring the broken monasteries.

I have a dream too

A dream of glorious paradise

Where the radiant sun shines

The peaceful moon smiles

Handsome stars wink

Happy flowers bloom

Prosperous rivers run

And the peaceful sky prevails.

These are my dreams

Dreams I am optimistic about

Dreams I see days and nights

Dreams I will live and die for.

Atlanta, GA, August 18, 2006

Note: *My visit to the historic Ebenezer Baptist Church where Dr. Martin Luther King Jr. served as a co-pastor inspired this poem. Dr. King's exemplary Nonviolence struggle and tremendous achievements inspired and strengthen my optimism for Dream Tibet.*

Tibet and the Titanic

Tibet and the Titanic

Same gigantic size

A significance of history

Yet, ignored by many

Tibet and the Titanic

Once a heavenly stage

A treasure of joy

Dream of millions

Tibet and the Titanic

Smashed by brutal forces

Killed in deep slumber

No rescue on-time

Tibet and the Titanic

Sank with profuse blood

Broke into many pieces

Rest in dust and rust

Tibet and the Titanic

Cemetery of fallen beings

Empty park for lonely spirits

Threshold of becoming extinct

Tibet and the Titanic

Items of a museum

Like mummies, earthen pots

And dinosaur skeletons

With time's passing by

Hope becomes thinner

For Tibet and the Titanic

As they crumble and disappear

With withering flowers

Exhausting energy

Failing good hearts

And piles of long decades.

Christmas Eve Mass for You

In the cool December air of festive celebrations

With colorful lightings that adorn the darkness
of the sky

The most beautiful Christmas Eve Mass I've
ever experienced

Thinking of you all, who are threatened if
celebrated.

The special Mass was filled with people and
good spirit

Of immense joy, peace, laughter, and prayers

I appeal to you, Lord Jesus with respect and full
heartedness

May you bless everyone to enjoy their religious
rights!

Why should one be a Christian to praise Jesus Christ?

Why should one ban Christians from celebrating Christmas?

Why should one force a religion onto other people?

I pray this Christmas Eve for those who are forbidden religion.

May you find friendship in the shower of bullets and explosives!

May you find peace inside broken and ransacked churches!

May you find happiness in high fever of warning and threats!

May Jesus be with you, and bless you forever on this Christmas Eve! Amen!

Christ the King, Kingston, RI. 24/12/11

Painful Anniversary

My heart flies afar

In the storm of bitterness,

With pieces of wounded spirits,

Of the deceased and survivors

My heart cries sadly,

Hearing the painful screams,

Feeling the numbing grief,

Remembering the tragedy

My heart chills,

In the ocean of tears,

Big swells of agony,

And waves of confusion

My heart crumbles,

Beneath ground zero,

With innocents' blood

And aspirations for peace

My heart wishes,

Rest for departed souls,

Blessings to ailing hearts,

Kindness in evil minds

My heart yearns,

For recovery from shock,

Restoration of inner peace,

Safety for human civilization

My heart is humbled,

With tribute to the innocents,

Respect for fire fighters,

Appreciation for forgiveness.

Trafalgar Way, Chamblee, GA 9/11/2006

The Torch of Torture

Entourage of the Olympic torch relay landed into town

The most beautiful city of San Francisco was afflicted

With wide ranges of emotions overcasting the open air

Many called that Olympic torch a '*Torch of Torture*'.

The splendid Bay Bridge witnessed unwavering courage

The Fishermen's Wharf hosted live spirits and willpower

Shedding tears and sweat the poor cried for betterment

Strong fists and yells soared from the other end of the bridge.

Pride of a majority collided with distress of minorities

Prosperity of a superpower challenged by destiny of the poor

Channels of propaganda confronted by peoples' own slogans

All Tibet demands is freedom from repression and genocide.

Fearing no giant communist that eclipsed modest peace

Diverse people from Africa to Asia lined up to protest

The entourage tried stealthy routes for a hush-hush sneak out

People crave to extinguish that flame of sin and brutality.

San Francisco, CA April 09, 2008

The Pink Lotus

In a small rising country called Burma located
adjacent to my motherland Tibet

A beautiful pink lotus flourishes bringing charm
to the shattered countryside

Her heart so brave and so beautiful shelters
dreams and hopes for dejected people

Her fragrance so nice and so pleasant purifies
polluted air induced by guns and tanks.

Sweet spirit of the lotus stands strongly
enduring decades of isolation and repression

Strong mind of the lotus proceeds so bravely
facing all kinds of storm and intimidation

Firm dedication of the lotus propels so stanchly
challenging one of the most ruthless regimes

Yet, she blossoms her petals so beautifully
provoking inspirations and hope for the
hopeless.

The native breeze that hits her strong through days and nights produces a whimper

Her whisper so calm yet so forceful easily surpasses the shooting noise of growing violence

Her radiance so wise and so bright glorifies the globe even as she was arrested and confined

She indeed is the pink lotus the entire planet should cherish sending all best wishes and support.

As the world knows, she posses no thorn but has glorious petals that smile and radiate peace

As the world knows, she enjoys no right but has insightful wisdom that surpasses selfish rulers

As the world knows, she hosts no greed but has resolute intentions that nurture peoples' hope

As the world knows, she raises no pride but has a Nobel Prize that honors her devotion for Peace.

Aung San Suu Kyi, the pink lotus, it is to you whom I offer my prayers and homage.

Burros and Boars

Willful Mexican Burros

And wild Texan Boars

that simply seek pleasure

believe never and ever

In boundaries manmade

Hate and discrimination

Hunger and intimidation

Endangering their lifespan

With massacres ordered

Hunting-guns loaded fully

Deadly machetes sharpened

and their homes deforested

Falling victims to pride

Facing persecution for revenge

Suffering mistreatment for greed

And bearing insults for no-good

I feel you poor Burros and Boars

I hear your heart-wrenching cries

I understand your credible fears

And I know you love your lives.

The Cemetery

Over the deep scary valley

Near the drying blue lake

There blazes a deep-red flame

That radiates sadness into the sky

The green leaves are saddened

Water birds are frightened

Frogs stare out in surprise and upset

People cry in sorrow and despair

There departs another old orphan

A witness to the Cultural Revolution

Her heart severely injured and broken

Her body cruelly abused and tortured

Last night in her dark little home

Village elders came to ease her journey

Lamas chanting Puja at high tone

Butter lamps lit on her altar

Struggling hard to breathe she lifts hands

Wrinkled and gnarled, to fold them for the last

Starring at the Dalai Lama's portrait

Peaceful and relaxed she looks, after all

A yogi led procession with white conch shell

Youngsters lift the body on their shoulder

Elders follow reciting *Om Mani Pedme Hum*

Together they walk to the lakeside crematory

Poor ragged body that lay on the pyre

Started sinking soon after setting afire

Smoke and consciousness fly far away

Ashes and relics conclude her life story

I wish her a rest from human cruelty

Hope she can join her parents at last

May her wishes for freedom be fulfilled soon!

Om Mani Pedme Hum, Om Mani Pedme Hum.

Note: Written after seeing another old Tibetan refugee, who escaped communist genocide in 1959, died after decades of hope, prayer and struggle.

Prayer Flags

Prayer flags are running

One direction to another

Where freedom is in tune

And gateways open warmly

Flags painting the sky beautiful

With colors that diversify truly

Bringing messages of inner peace

Sharing a mantra of infinite love

Wind flying prayer flags high

Projects their heartfelt message

Wish everyone could feel their spirit

Who craves freedom.

I am Wind

I am wind who enforces life

I am wind who infuses power

I am wind who nourishes minds

I am wind who connects all.

I am wind who rejects confinement

I am wind who dislikes prejudice

I am wind who confronts discrimination

I am wind who disapproves covertness.

I am wind who heaves through ruptures

I am wind who pushes off veiling clouds

I am wind who humbles arrogant trees

I am wind who pacifies the blazing sun.

I am wind who opts for transparency

I am wind who aspires for simplicity

I am wind who strives for positivity

I am wind who whispers for eco-friendly.

I am wind who believes in love

I am wind who fights for justice

I am wind who flies for freedom

I am wind who gusts for peace.

The Invincible Heart

Censorship

Repression

Prohibition

Intimidation

Allegation

Separation

Detention

Dissuasion

Persecution

But, can they?

Arrest

Encage

Isolate

Restrain

Denounce

Detach

Disfigure

Defeat

Or assassinate

The heart

The soul

The spirit

The source

Really?

III. Love &

Life

Sketch on My Heart

Choosing over a plain paper

I sketch my fond feeling deep within

For my heart is blessed and safe

untouched by fire and hailstorms

Sweet feeling for you is lively

rising inside like a waxing moon

each breath I take pumps in

fresh heartbeats that call for you.

My love and warmth for you

can't be swamped by a river

a sea wave or even by a hurricane

For it's the innermost of my heart

where I carve and cherish love.

It glows and thrives

every minute, every hour, for you

until my final pulse wanes away

I have sketched an eternal feeling

 that binds us strong in heart forever.

I am Gone Too Far

Come on back, my Guru says

Get back to home, my mother pleads

How are you man? My friends ask

But, I am gone, gone too far

I am in a peaceful city, by the way

Spending everyday, almost, alone

Sitting hours in B.P. Library, I read

Stories of people gone far like me

I can hear you all only by phone, today

I can imagine you all waving at me

I can feel generous blessings you send

But I am far, gone too far away

Often, I get some great opportunities--

To meditate, talk and play with you all

Wish I could do this beyond daydreams

But, I know, I am far, gone too far

Sometimes, my cheeks are wet

Other times, my heart is heavy

Hope you all don't hear my cries

No worries, I am far, gone far away

I am afraid we may not see each other again

Never ever, at least, in this lifetime

Not that I would forget or forsake you now

But, because I am gone, gone too far

Some great paths are a circle

Like one that brings Columbus back

But, afraid my trail may be a narrow tunnel

So, there is no return once I set forth

I confess, I am gone, gone too far

From noble land of Buddha and my lamas

I keep my mind calm and pure

Although, I am gone, gone far away.

Berkeley City Library, CA

My Father's Advice for Life

Do not fight for power like a king

Do not strive for fame like a fool

Do not crave for wealth like a miser

Be ready to help like a yak

Do not be prideful like an eagle

Do not be vicious like a snake

Do not be suspicious like a rabbit

Be ready to help like a yak

Do not gossip endlessly like a parrot

Do not eat carelessly like a pig

Do not breathe lazily like a donkey

Be ready to help like a yak

Do not get excited like a rooster

Do not get worried like a coyote

Do not lose virtue like a skunk

Be ready to help like a yak

Do not breed enmity like a scorpion

Do not forget kindness like a vulture

Do not forsake home like a dinosaur

Be simple, and enjoy life like a yak.

My Mother

In the midst of the twinkling stars
The bright moon, you smile
I'm reminded of my mother
Whenever I chance to see you.

The colorful rainbow
That appears in the sprinkled sky
So curved and so wrinkled
Seems to be my poor mother
Whenever I chance to stare at you.

The sweetest song that came
From the topmost part of the mango tree
Holy teachings
That are given by His Holiness
And the melodious voice produced
By the native guitar of Sarasvati,
All these, remind me of my mother's voice.

I came to know your kindness

I can smell your handmade food delicious

I wish and pray for your welfare

Only now, when you're far far

Away from me.

Mundgod, Karnataka State, India 1998

It's Time to Move!

February is approaching fast
Flowers are budding out
Butterflies are flying around
It's time for me to move

Bees are humming about
Lovers are singing high
Broken-hearts are crying loud
It's time for me to move

Pollens are afflicting air
Allergies are causing headaches
Peach blossoms are falling soon
It's time for me to move

Wind is swooshing stronger
Waves are building higher
Rocks are standing firmer
It's time for me to move

Streets are getting noisier

Tremors are expected anytime

Calmness is fading out

It's time for me to move

Morning fog is blocking vision

Daytime smog is creating mirage

Evening cold is chilling spines

It's time for me to move

Distress is harsh to experience

Memories are hard to erase

Happiness is right to live

It's time for me to move.

Bonar Street, Berkeley, CA Feb. 09

My Fragile Footprints

Playful Western Summer

Facing a cool sea-breeze I walk on the beautiful
Pacific shore

Moving further I leave consecutive footprints on
golden sand

Looking around I see many people surfing on
uneven waves

While others enjoy sunbaths, their eyes
following my path.

Feeling curious and awkward I turn backward to
assess the moment

I watch my footprints as a strong wave rushes
ashore

Footprints are erased and sand-grains are
dragged deep into the ocean

For reasons I don't know, and perhaps better not
to know ever.

Colorful Eastern Fall

Walking into the colorful woods I saw
butterflies fluttering around

Attracted by their charming nature I wanted to
roam as far and free

Following their uncertain path left me clueless

Struggling for a long time I sneaked out of the
alluring deception and mystery.

Turning back from a freeway I saw my dream
and illusion crumble

With withering leaves that fell and covered
trails others and I took

Fantasy of lovely trees and playful butterflies
turned into a skeleton park

The wind blowing dead-leaves all over
reminded me of a foggy destiny.

White Northern Winter

My longing for snowfall turned into excitement
for sledding and skiing

Braving cold winds and heavy snowstorms I
walked onto a deserted hill

The further I stride out the more footprints I left
onto the snow field

With prayers I hoped my Guru could trace me
down if I got lost in gloom.

Each footprint gets buried under new layers of
snow and freezing ice

Yet looking backward would bear nothing more
than pain and distress

Keeping faith in my mind and warmth in my
body I pursue an expedition of life

The blizzard may bury me as well as my
footprints transient by nature.

Green Southern Spring

The moist spring field was lit up by warm sun
for aroma and fresh plants

Fascinating tulips and other flowers' blooms
robbed me of a childish mind

Melodies of singing birds and hymning insects
besieged mumbling chants

The season's so heavenly that I feel hesitant to
afflict it with stinky footprints.

With excitement in their hearts the migratory
birds return to their hometown north

Jumping into the sky I flapped my hands to see
if I can fly away with geese

Falling down onto delicate ground I pressed
another set of fragile footprints

Cherishing flowers I walk towards the ocean to
refresh and reset my vision afar.

Narragansett, RI

Its Gonna Be Cold

The flowers are fading
The grasses are graying
The wind is blowing high
Its gonna be cold.

The leaves are falling down
The hailstorms rushing forward
The birds are fleeing away
Its gonna be cold.

The road is icing up
The playgrounds are getting empty
The blizzard is approaching
Its gonna be cold.

My friends are staying back
I am moving far north
But, don't you worry my dear friends
For its gonna be cold.

Your thoughts keep me warm, always.
Although its gonna be cold.
Atlanta, GA 12/2010

Congratulations!

I greet you respectfully

And congratulate you

On your Graduation Day

With showers of praise

And petals of cheers

For your eternal faith

Unshakable commitment

Surpassing challenges

Unlimited dedications

And for the prolific achievement

Congratulations my friend

I adore you much!

The Pretty Leaf I Cherish

That coldest damn fall-night

In the darkness off Anita Street

When colorful leaves met on the ground

The wind blew away that pretty leaf

Whom I cherished deep in my tender heart

I came back home in the darkness

Saddened and disappointed as I could be

Night's sleep and day's smile all upset

Since my soul missed that hearty leaf

And wondered if she missed me alike

I shouldn't be on their path anyways

Had both the leaf and wind concurred

Thus, I sent my invisible warm-prayers

For I wish happiness to the adorable angel

One who's divinely sweet and beautiful

I can be sad but never become a wind

For the only reason *I wish to force nobody*

Good luck with you my beloved pretty leaf

And remember I wish you happy always

No matter whether you fly south or north.

I Give It Up

'Make me like you more'

That's what an angel told me

I was stunned that moment

For I really don't know how

To value and endure such

Love that is conditional

Yet I tried, tried hard

To appease that angel

Not to entice her selfishly

But to hold her close

For my heart loves her

No, never for wealth or degree

In days' and nights' dreams

I waited for her applause

Like that of two happy hands

That bring cheer to my soul

Months passed by in hope

Seasons took a turn in colors

Trees shed their gilded leaves

Thus, I tore my heart down

With silent drops of tears

And hidden layers of scars

Today, I mourn you angel

I give up, I give it up!

Highway 108

The sky was getting dark

The wind was blowing cold

Cars were rushing fast

People were fading away

She was headed south

And I was destined north

We waved at each other

As we stood on the same path

Watching out for each other

Smiling at each other

Thinking of each other

Wishing for each other

On that Highway 108

Covered by darkness

Yet, lighted with hope

Adorned with prayers, Safe travels!

Wet Lips

It's not the ocean mist

Nor the drizzling rain

Its you, young lady

Who wet my lips

With lips full of nectar

With eyes full of emotion

And a heart full of love

Its you, young lady

Who wet my lips.

The Great Swamp

Every evening when I ride my bike by you,
Great Swamp

I witness something different appearing on your
face

Sometimes you wear orange rays that the
fading-sun emits

And at times you echo hostile lightening the
upset sky expresses.

Great Swamp, you reflect the cool and beautiful
moon sometimes

And, you host romantic swans so kindly every
day and night

Pure and delicate lilies display their full
blossom in you often

But you look sad and lonely sometimes with no
one around.

In spring, Great Swamp, you carry images of
fresh tree leaves

And, in the summer you adorn your home with flowers and happy fishes

The fall reflects absolute on your face with burgundy, pink, and gold

But the winter shuts your window with chunks of frozen ice.

Oh Great Swamp, you grow old witnessing positives and negatives

And you endure the brunt of unpredictable weather and emotional flux

As I stop pedaling intended to look at you over the wooden bridge

It's you who mirrors my own face and soul - vivid and perfect.

The historic Great Swamp, Kingston, RI

See You Daddy

Landing after flying,

Waning after waxing,

Withering after blooming,

Fading after growing,

Vacant after occupation,

Sunset after sunrise,

Darkness after daylight,

Death after birth.

The world goes around.

Flying after landing,

Waxing after waning,

Blooming after withering,

Growing after fading,

Occupation after vacant,

Sunrise after sunset,

Daylight after darkness,

Birth after death.

See you daddy,

I pray for you!

Boston, MA 2012

Ocean, My Spirit

It brings me an immense calm to sit by the
ocean

As I know my ancestors' spirits reside in it

Their souls the Himalayas became a river of
tears

And altogether they fall and rest inside the
ocean

Meeting by the ocean I can feel and hear my
ancestors

Patting on my head and whispering into my ears

"Grandson" they called and embrace me so
dearly

As if they find a missing piece of their hearty
spirit

I am proud to see the openness of my ancestral spirit

And the depth of their insightful wisdom and love

The waves of their eternal courage and willpower

And the warmth they share with every sentient being

I wanna soak my feet deep into the great ocean

I wanna cherish their spirit warm inside my heart

I wanna unfurl their dreams high with good wishes

And, I wanna offer my spirit wholly to the ocean.

May 15, 2011 Narragansett, RI

Union in One Good Heart

Far away in the desert of California
I see orange rays connecting earth and sky
It is my turn to play the naughty sun
And yours to be the peaceful moon.

You smile in the clear Californian sky
And I laugh above the foothills of Himalaya
No matter how long we dream and struggle
Together we reside in one a good heart.

Far away I see a cluster of twinkling lights
Yet, you the full-moon surpass others
Thus, I keep staring at you constantly
In the rear mirror of the Chevy Van.

Highway CA 58 continues to mingle in the dark
My dream becomes more and more vivid
Together we'll spend our life in meaning,
The moment the sun rises from the eastern horizon.

Acknowledgements

Ever since I was born into this world, I enjoy unconditional love, immense kindness, genuine friendship, enlightening wisdom, and immeasurable compassion from many women and men of our planet earth. I am very grateful to all of them for blessing me with generous contributions, thoughtful inspirations, and positive attitudes. I am also very grateful to other sentient beings, who I do not personally know, for their indirect roles and anonymous support in making my world more harmonious, vibrant and wholesome.

My special respect and appreciation to many compassionate spiritual masters and their tutors at the Drepung Loseling Monastery, caring professors at the University of Rhode Island, my late father Mr. Chonga Tsering and mother

Mrs. Choney Dolma, teachers, family, friends and well-wishers shining throughout the globe.

I will not be able to share this book today without the kindness of Dr. Lou Fuerstman, Eleanor Hand, Dr. Geshe Lobsang Tenzin Negi and Dr. Art Stein. I extend my heartfelt gratitude to Dr. Paul Bueno de Mesquita of the URI Center for Nonviolence & Peace Studies for publishing this poetry book and Kathryn Lee Johnson for editing the poems. I dedicate all merits accumulated to universal peace!

Thupten Tendhar